The Kurly Sue Story

Written by Kayo Fraser

Illustrated by Bonnie Shields

Seed of Light
255 N Boulder Rd
Deer Lodge, MT 59722
406-846-3686
www.seedoflight.com

Cover illustrations by Bonnie Shields
Published in association with:
Keokee Books of Sandpoint, Idaho
www.keokeebooks.com

Book design by Keokee Books
Softcover edition ISBN: 979-8-9913442-0-3
Printed in the United States of America

Dedication

This book is dedicated to everyone who has rescued animals and provided them with a loving home.

Special thanks to my friends and family for encouraging me to publish my stories.

Foreword

"The Kurly Sue Story" is the first book in the Animal Spirit Series, a collection of true stories about animals with hidden tales that deserve to be told. Sometimes, these stories can be uncovered through a professional Animal Communicator.

During a communication session, Kurly Sue's past was revealed, and the author dives deep into the adventures that followed.

These stories are non-fiction, enriched with creative insights.

Chapter 1

The wind whipped through my tight gray curls as I braced myself in the back of the old red pickup truck. The chill of the cold and cloudy November day made me wish I had stayed in the barn where it was warm. The wind blew the fur on my face into my eyes but all I could see was a long ribbon of road stretching across the high desert of Wyoming. I just stared out the back of the truck, looking at where we had been. I didn't know what had gone wrong with my life. Lonely and confused, I had to do something, even if it was scary.

I had never ridden in the back of a truck before, and the blurring speed was terrifying. My judgment may have been clouded by my fear, but my desire to escape prodded me to leap from the truck. I flew into the windy, steel-gray sky.

The highway was a running blur as I soared through the air. The earth came up to meet me with a hard whack! I bumped and bounced and spun around and around until I rolled into some sagebrush. I was not sure if I was alive or dead, or somewhere in between. I could only lie there alongside the road in a stupor.

Memories rushed through my mind's eye like a movie as I recalled happier days when I was at home with My Lady.

She was soft and warm, and when I curled up in her lap, she stroked my head and gently rubbed my ears. I would fall asleep with a smile in my heart.

Her once-dark hair was now streaked with gray and pulled back into a bun. She loved me as much as I loved her.

Sometimes during the summer, she would get too busy working in the garden and mowing grass. But by evening we would sit in the shade, watch the clouds drift by, and smell the air. The sweet fragrance of flowers and freshly cut grass made me happy to be alive. A slight breeze cooled the heat from the sun. I thought of this as wind-shine.

During the winter we would sit by the wood-burning stove, cuddled under a blanket to stay warm. I liked these times even better than summer because we had little else to do but be together and listen to the fire crackle in the stove.

I loved My Lady like she was my very own mother. She fed me twice a day. I didn't think she gave me enough food, but she said something about "not getting too fat," whatever that meant.

Pizza was our favorite food, but I liked French fries a lot. My Lady always shared her food with me. Every time we'd go to town, I could hardly wait to see what treats would come from the drive-up food place. I would run from window to window in eager expectation. Sometimes she would holler at me to sit still, but I loved to eat—no matter what it was—and I couldn't contain myself.

Some days we would play my favorite game, "Catch me if you can." I'd run around the room teasing My Lady to chase me, but just before she caught me, I'd dart in the other direction barking and laughing as I ran. It was so much fun! When I became tired, I'd let her catch me and pick me up in her warm arms. There was always a treat for me at the end of the game, so I'd let her believe she won!

4

Chapter 2

A wave of pain flooded my body and brought me back to reality. My bruised muscles ached, and my hip hurt from the impact of the ground, but the real pain, buried deep inside my soul, was far worse than the physical pain. It clouded my brain.

Slowly I opened my eyes, and the world seemed to spin around. I was afraid and shivered from the cold reality of what I had just done. The roar of passing cars and trucks zipped by not far from where I fell. I heard the sounds but couldn't make sense of the danger I was in.

To stop the confusion, I closed my eyes and remembered the man who had kidnapped me. I tried to wiggle free from his captive hands. I barked for My Lady to help me, but the man shook me and told me to be still. Holding me tightly, he left the house then tossed me onto the front seat of his truck.

"Now, stay there and shut up!" he shouted, as he put the truck in gear and sped away. I ran to the window and barked as loudly as I could for My Lady. "Help!"

We drove for a long time. When the truck finally stopped moving, the man opened the door, and I bolted out. I didn't care where we were; I just had to get out.

"Well, here is where you live now, mutt," he said with a snarl. "Better get used to it."

I didn't understand. His voice was harsh, and my name wasn't Mutt. There was something familiar about him, but I couldn't remember where I'd heard his voice before.

This was a very strange place with lots of different smells. There were several barns and outbuildings. Beyond that was nothing but tall grass as far as I could see. I would have investigated them if I hadn't been so desperate to figure out what had happened to me.

Hoping to be safe and warm, I tried to follow the man into the house, but he slammed the door in my face and shouted, "Stay outside!"

His sharp commands frightened and confused me. I had always lived with My Lady and couldn't understand why the man had taken me away. Where was My Lady? What was this place? Why was I here?

Three large dogs came over to sniff me. I wanted to be friends, but I was not sure they did. One was a border collie named June. She was nice to me. She tried to explain about life here, "on the ranch" as she called it, but she didn't know why I was here, so my questions

went unanswered. She told me her job was to protect the sheep and move them from pasture to pasture. There were many animals around the ranch I had not seen before, and "sheep" must have been one of them.

Rusty, a red heeler, and Bandit, a blue heeler, snarled at me. They told me they were very busy and had no time to mess with a spoiled "city" dog. They trotted away to "tend to some very important business," I heard them say.

"They work the cattle," June told me. Whatever "cattle" meant.

Just before darkness set in, the door to the house opened, and the man who kidnapped me put down several dishes with interesting-smelling food. All the dogs came running and jumping in the air. He set a dish in front of each dog, including me. It was the first food I'd had all day, and I ate it fast and furiously.

After our meal, I checked everyone's bowl, but there was not even a lick left for me to clean up. My Lady always let me clean her plate. She called it "pre-wash."

June told me to find a warm place to sleep in the barn. "Stay away from the cats. They don't like dogs, and if you get too close to them, they'll swat your nose with sharp claws," June warned. I didn't know what "cats" were, but I saw a small, fluffy creature, and when I tried to smell it, it hissed at me and swatted my nose. "Ouch," I yelped. This must be a "cat". I vowed to stay clear of all cats forever.

It was cold in the barn, even in the hay, and no one would let me sleep next to them. June slept with the sheep and the other two dogs snapped at me when I tried to get close to their warm bodies. My life had changed, and there was nothing I could do about it right then, so I curled up in the hay and fell fast asleep. I was tired from my confusing day. Tomorrow I would try to figure things out, I promised myself.

When morning came, so did more curious critters. There were birds that couldn't fly; June called them "chickens". It was fun to chase them and listen to them squawk until a mother hen came running at me with her wings flapping. She pecked me on my behind, "Get out of here and leave my chicks alone," she cackled. At least that was what I figured she said. I didn't speak chicken any better than I spoke cat, but there was no mistaking the body language.

B. Shedley
CCI

"Fine!" I told her. "I wasn't going to hurt them, I just wanted to play."

The days and nights came and went. Everyone seemed to have a job except me. I felt useless, alone, and lost. The cats chased mice and didn't like me in their way. The other dogs were too busy to talk with me. Chickens were off-limits, and the people who lived in the house didn't care about me. I needed to find something I could do to keep busy.

One day it looked like the cows were getting too close to the yard by the barn. Neither Rusty nor Bandit were around, so I thought I would try to help. Maybe the other dogs would like me when they saw how useful I could be. I ran under the barbed wire fence in a flash, "Shoo, shoo! Get out of here!" I barked at the cows.

B. Shields

Taken by surprise, the cow in the front turned and ran in the other direction, away from the gate by the barn. I found out, when the lead cow turns, all the cows turn. I hadn't noticed that Rusty and Bandit were in the back trying to push them through the gate.

Soon there was a dusty cloud of confusion. The ranch dogs tried to persuade the cows to re-enter the barnyard, not knowing I was talking them into leaving. When they heard my high-pitched bark, they came running at me. At first, I thought they were going to thank me, but instead, Rusty charged toward me and snapped at my nose, sending me head-first into the middle of a warm, smelly pile of fresh, green cow poop. Kerplop!

I was shocked! My pride was hurt a lot more than my body. I didn't understand why Rusty was so mad at me until I saw the man raise his arms and usher the cows into the barnyard. I had made a mistake.

I liked the fresh scent on my coat, but it was too thick and matted my fur. I rolled in the clean brown grass to remove some of the sticky poop, but there was nothing I could do about my new shame. It was another sign of rejection and humiliation. I had just wanted to fit in, but now, all the dogs looked at me in disgust, even June, who had been so nice to me before.

My mood couldn't have gotten any darker than it was right then. Everything I tried to do at the ranch got me in trouble. I just wanted to get lost in my deepest thoughts and remember the life I once had—a life that was gone forever.

Chapter 3

One day June told me about Thanksgiving.

"It's a day the people celebrate with lots of food," she said. "After they eat, they bring out a platter of turkey scraps, gravy, and dressing for us dogs. It's a great day, and we are thankful for the scrumptious food!"

I remember eating turkey with My Lady. It was deee-licious!

Different people started coming to the ranch each day - big people and small people. New smells floated out of the door when it opened. The aromas of freshly baked bread and pumpkin-spiced pies made me drool.

Laughter danced through the house and spilled out into the barnyard. People were happy. I wanted to be happy too, but it seemed hopeless.

On that day, some of the men had to make a trip to town and all the large dogs hopped in the back of the red pickup truck eager for the adventure.

One of the visiting kids picked me up and tossed me in the back of the truck, too. I had never been in the back of a truck before, and it was exhilarating! The other dogs barked as music drifted from the front of the truck, adding to the excitement.

It was a long way to town and the air was very cold. The long tight curls on my body helped to keep me warm, but the cold that ran deep inside my soul made me shiver.

"I don't belong here," I told June. "I want to find My Lady."

June said, "No, no. You don't need to go. Stay here with us. Things will get better. You don't want to miss out on the turkey and gravy in a couple of days."

"I've got to try to find her," I said. The sorrow was so heavy in my heart that I acted without thinking. As the scenery flew by, I leapt from the back of the truck into the cold wind.

June barked and barked to tell her humans that I had jumped from the truck, but no one had noticed.

"Be safe!" June barked. "Be Safe." There wasn't much else she could say.

That's how I ended up on the endless road, confused, and in pain. My head hurt. My hips ached from the fall, but the lost, hopeless feeling deep inside me was far worse.

Chapter 4

The roar of passing cars and trucks was deafening as they zipped by, not far from where I lay. Suddenly all was quiet. I opened my eyes and could hardly believe what I saw in front of me! Standing there in the sagebrush was My Lady!

She was surrounded by bright light—like an angel! Maybe I had died and gone to heaven. I was so happy to find My Lady; nothing else mattered.

My Lady knelt beside me and softly stroked the curls on my body. My tail wagged. That was the only part of my body that didn't hurt.

She said, "You went looking for me, didn't you, my precious little puppy?

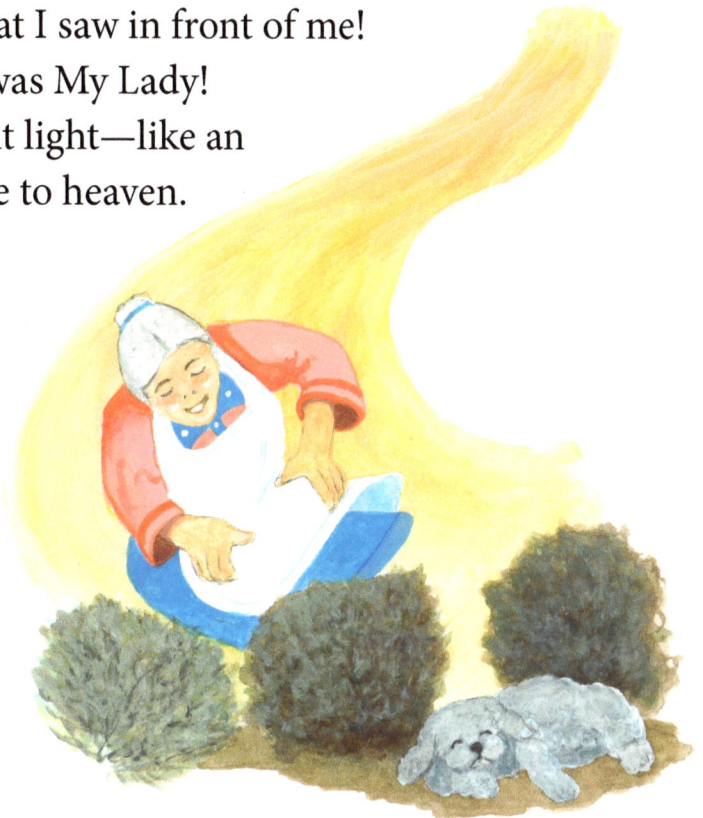

You will not be able to join me, because I died. I went to be with my husband Charlie who died before you came to live with me. I missed him very much, as I miss you now, but I couldn't go see him until it was my time. It is not your time yet, to join us."

She went on to explain in her soothing voice, "It was my son who took you to live with his family on their ranch. I had hoped you would like it there. But worry not my little pet; I will help you find another home. You have many wonderful adventures ahead of you."

My Lady's voice trailed away as she faded from sight. The joy of seeing her gave me a little hope, but I was very sad to know that I would not live with My Lady ever again. At least I had found the answers I needed, and I understood why I was taken from my home and the person I had loved.

I remember the strange quiet in our home the day I was taken away. I thought My Lady had slept in but, she wouldn't wake up when I asked to go outside. Something was different about her. I didn't understand at the time that My Lady had died.

People came, and I heard them cry. I didn't know them very well because I had always stayed close to My Lady when they visited. I remembered the scent and the voices of the people who came, including the man who took me away.

As I lay alone in the desert, I was not sure my decision to jump out of the truck had been a wise one. But it was a decision I had to live with.

Not knowing what else to do, I finally stood up, shook myself, and slowly walked in the same direction the truck had been traveling. I decided to go forward because there was no reason to go back. But I couldn't help but worry about my future.

I walked and walked and walked. Night came, and so did the snow that had threatened all day. I curled up under some sagebrush, tucked my nose under my legs, and fell into a fitful sleep.

The morning's sky was still dreary. I felt like I was living in a terrible dream, but the hunger and cold were real. I licked the wet snow, which quenched my thirst, but there was nothing to eat, so the only thing to do was walk some more - to where I did not know.

I lost track of how long I'd been lost in the desert. Maybe it was two days, but it seemed like an eternity. The cold ran deep inside of me, and the loneliness was so heavy I could hardly lift my head. There were no houses around. I didn't know how I would find a new home. All I could do was walk.

I knew My Lady was always nearby. I couldn't see her or hear her, but I could feel her presence.

Most of the new snow melted by midday, leaving just enough to lick for water. I thought maybe this was the Thanksgiving Day June told me about. I wondered if I had done the right thing by leaving the ranch. I missed the comfort of the sweet-smelling hay in the barn where I could at least curl up to stay warm. I also missed the delicious meals every day. But even the gnawing hunger I felt, with all my other pain, was better than living a life where I was not happy, wanted, or needed.

It was getting dark again and I dreaded spending another night alone in the desert. The other dogs on the ranch were probably eating leftover turkey, and here I was – wet, cold, and hungry. I found a dead chipmunk in the grass. It must have tried to cross the road at the wrong time and was hit by a car. I thought about eating it, but the smell nauseated me.

Suddenly, I heard the voice of My Lady shout, "Here they come! Here they come!"

"Who? Who is coming?" I asked, feeling a little dazed, but curious.

"The people who will give you a wonderful home!" My Lady said.

"Who? Where? Where? Who are they?" I asked, almost afraid to be excited.

"Come closer to the road so they can see you," My Lady said.

"Where are they? I don't see them."

"See the truck and horse trailer? They are The People! You will meet them soon."

Chapter 5

A white one-ton pick-up truck pulling a very large white six-horse trailer sped down the lonely stretch of highway. Fritz, the man behind the wheel, had been driving for ten hours and was anxious to get to the horse sale in Rock Springs, Wyoming. Traveling on Thursday, Thanksgiving Day, was necessary because the sale started Friday.

Liz, a small middle-aged woman, sat half asleep, on the passenger side of the truck. She was Fritz's wife and was eager to arrive at the sale if for no other reason than to get out of the truck and stretch her legs. The light was fading, but it was not quite dark.

Not knowing why, Liz glanced at the other side of the road. In the dusky light, she barely saw a scruffy little dog sniffing at some roadkill.

"Puppy!" She shouted with concern in her voice.

"Was it alive? Or dead?" Fritz asked.

"It was alive!" she replied.

Fritz raised his foot from the gas pedal and slowly applied the brakes to the truck. By the time he was able to slow the truck and trailer down from 60 miles per hour to pull safely off the road onto the desert shoulder, he had traveled almost half a mile. He got out of the truck and walked back, looking for the little dog his wife had seen. Fritz was a tall man with long, lean legs that were accustomed to walking fast. He had seen no houses around for miles and knew the closest town was 30 miles away in either direction.

"Why was there a little dog out here in the middle of nowhere?" he asked himself out loud. "I hope I can catch it. I sure would hate to leave it out here on the highway at night. It might get run over."

Fritz had walked quite a distance but could not see a dog ahead of him. Traffic was picking up on this narrow, two-lane road; semi-trucks with their trailers raced by with a stumbling breeze. The light had faded fast, so regrettably, Fritz turned around and headed back to his truck.

When he arrived at his trailer, a white Suburban pulled up in front of him. Liz went out to meet the people in the car to let them know they didn't need help. People in the West often stopped to help someone if they were stranded on the side of the road. It's what they still do.

The window rolled down and a well-dressed man held up a shaggy, wet, and very dirty, little poodle and asked, "Is this your dog? We saw your truck and trailer parked and a man walking then saw the dog and figured it was yours."

The people in the Suburban were nicely dressed. They were probably traveling home from a Thanksgiving dinner somewhere. The muddy dog looked out of place in their clean car.

"No." Fritz explained, "We are headed for Rock Springs, and my wife saw it on the road. We were worried about it being out here all alone. I walked as far as I could before I thought I should head back."

The man who held the dog said the Humane Society in their town was closed until Monday, but the one in Rock Springs stayed open all weekend, and that would be a good place to take the dog.

"Well, we stopped to help it, but I wasn't sure it would even let me catch it if I did find it. Thanks for picking it up; we will take care of it from here," Fritz told them.

Liz pulled a blanket from the trailer and wrapped it around the stinky, wet dog. There was a distinct odor of cow manure and dead animals emitting from this tiny canine package.

The little dog hardly moved a muscle as she slept.

"I hope she's not sick," Liz said. "She hasn't moved an inch since she's been here."

B. SHIELDS
C C I

After what seemed like a long time, warmth finally filled the little dog's body, and she kissed the woman's hand to show her gratitude for the kindness.

"Oh!" Liz said to her husband. "She just licked my hand! I think she will be okay now."

It was dark when Fritz and Liz finally arrived in Rock Springs. They parked the horse trailer and plugged it into the electricity at the fairgrounds where the sale would take place. It was too cold to make the little dog sleep in the back of the trailer, so Fritz made a bed next to him in the sleeper. "We can call the Humane Society tomorrow," he said.

For the next three days, Fritz and Liz were busy with the sale and didn't have a chance to make that call. They shared their meals with the hungry little guest and took turns walking her using a piece of bailing twine for a leash. It didn't take long for the little dog to accept them as friends and eagerly went with them wherever they took her.

After spending three days with this gray ball of fur, Fritz knew he would never call the Humane Society. On their last night in town, they decided to stay in a motel room where Fritz gave their new little friend a much-needed bath.

"What do you think we should call her?" he asked his wife.

Many names passed their lips. Gypsy? Road Tramp? Traveler? Highway? They ran through the alphabet trying out girl names, but nothing seemed to fit.

It was hard to tell the little dog's breed because her eyes were hidden behind a mass of curly hair. She looked like a poodle and terrier mix. "She sure is curly!" Liz said. "That's it! We will call her Kurly Sue."

Life changed that day. Kurly Sue found a home where she belonged again. Kurly Sue still missed "My Lady" sometimes, but she was too busy now to think about it very much. She had lots to do, the cats didn't swat at her if she sniffed them, and the other animals were nice to her. In the evenings each dog got a special treat, one at a time. She had a warm bed to sleep in, but most importantly, she had two people who loved her as much as she loved them.

Kurly Sue learned it was worth taking a risk to find happiness.

She said, "We dogs have a lot to teach you humans, especially about slowing down and savoring life instead of rush, rush, rushing through it always trying to achieve something. You can achieve things sometimes simply by Be-ing instead of Do-ing. If people paced themselves and slowed down a little, they could enjoy the wind-shine."

The End

"We are not sure when Kurly Sue was born but
she was part of our family from 2002 to 2007.
We still miss her."

Kayo Fraser, Author

Kayo Fraser lives in Montana with her husband, Alex. Animals have always played an important role in their lives, including cats, dogs, and horses. Kayo discovered her passion for creative writing in junior high school and has continued with journal writing and free verse poetry since then. She has attended several writing workshops and founded a writing group called "Women Writing for Fun and Therapy."

Kayo has contributed articles to numerous equestrian magazines and published an annual directory called "The Reach" for ten years, helping people find breeders and businesses that support the draft horse and driving horse industries. Her greatest joy comes from bringing to life the characters that inhabit her imagination.

Her first novel, "Listen to Your Spirit", was published by Raven Publishing. While the main characters are human, the essence of the story revolves around a spirit animal in the form of a black leopard. She writes primarily for young readers, but her books appeal to people of all ages and backgrounds.

Kayo's second book, "And God Says, 'Yes'", is being republished and will be available soon. The opening sentence reads, "Imagine you are traveling the Universe with God."

Kayo thinks outside conventional boundaries and presents her topics for readers to explore new realms. In addition to writing, she enjoys photography and buying and selling antiques. Together with her husband, she owns and operates the Fraser School of Driving, where they teach people how to drive horses to carts, wagons, and carriages.

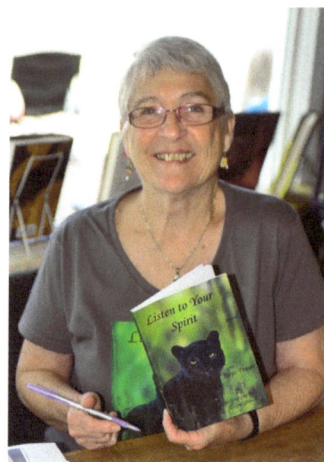

Bonnie Shields, Illustrator

Bonnie has been a full-time professional artist since 1973, and she is best known as the official Tennessee Mule Artist. After moving West, her art expanded, and she found success working with Leanin' Tree, the largest publisher of Western greeting cards.

Bonnie has sculpted mules and draft horses for bronze pieces and has illustrated books for many well-known authors, including Marguerite Henry's "Brown Sunshine" and Meredith Hodges's "Jasper: The Story of a Mule," along with a collection of related books and a DVD. Meredith, the owner of Lucky Three Productions, L.L.C., created a comprehensive coffee table book showcasing Bonnie Shields's work, which you can find here: www.luckythreeranchstore.com.

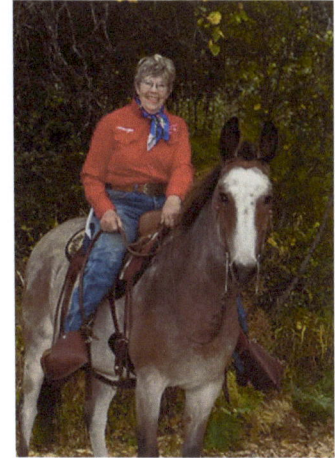

As an award-winning artist, Bonnie has designed buckles, posters, and covers for various publications. She is a charter member of Cowboy Cartoonists International and has served on their board, as well as being involved with the American Donkey and Mule Society.

Currently, Bonnie resides in Sandpoint, Idaho, where she continues to paint and illustrate books. We are honored to have Bonnie Shields illustrate "The Kurly Sue Story."

Visit her website at: www.bonnieshields.com

www.ingramcontent.com/pod-product-compliance
Lightning Source LLC
Chambersburg PA
CBHW041427090426
42741CB00002B/73

9798991344203